It Ends With Me

www.PeacePresidentUnited.org
www.DiscoverCHA.org

It Ends With Me

A Loving Meditation on
Parenting, Presence, and Healing

PEACE PRESIDENT

Peace President United Publishing
Planet Earth

It Ends With Me

Peace President United Publishing
Planet Earth

© 2026 Peace President United
All rights reserved. No part of this book may be
reproduced in any manner without the written permission
from the author and publisher.

ISBN: 978-0-9862276-7-7
Printed in the United States of America

*To the ones who came before,
who did the best they could
with what they were taught.
And to the ones who come after—
may you carry only what's true.*

*The deepest wounds a child carries
are those of an unhealed parent.*

*What I inherited was
often unattended sorrow and pain.*

*Yet, what I am is unconditional love.
The wounds continue only if I carry them.*

*Though love was never broken—
only veiled, waiting to be remembered.*

*The patterns end with me.
For I AM the unending presence illuminated
within and without.*

*Everpresent timeless grace—
Infinite Loving Awareness.*

Contents

Preface

xv

Introduction

xxi

1. Inheritance of Wounds

29

2. Recognition and Reverence

35

3. The Mirror and the Self

42

4. The Sacred Undoing
45

5. The Healing Spiral
52

6. Love as Presence
58

7. The Guest We Cannot Keep
63

8. Like the Sun Loves the Flower
71

9. The Flame Inside the Form
77

10. The Door is Still Open
83

11. What If I Don't Know
91

12. It Ends With Me
99

Contents

About the Author
109

Other Books by Peace President
112

Acknowledgments
113

Before any story begins,
there is the one who lives it.

The quiet pulse behind every thought.
The witness behind every feeling.
The presence that never leaves.

This book is called *It Ends With Me*.
But the ME spoken of here is not
the small one shaped by fear or memory.
Not the name you were given.
Not the roles you carry.

It Ends With Me

Not the false identities
you innocently believe you are.

ME is Mysterious Existence.
(M - mysterious, E - existence, ME)

The living truth that breathes
through every moment,
even when you forget to notice.

When I look at what I truly am,
I find no edges.
No clear beginning.
No clear ending.

Only a presence that keeps unfolding,
learning, unlearning,
dancing and singing through
the strange beauty of being alive.

Mysterious Existence moves
through glories and confusion,
through wonder and ache,
through the quiet and the chaos,
and it keeps whispering
that none of this is happening to us.

It is happening as us.

Preface

Life plays,
and "we" play with it... as it.

For we *are* the dance and the dancer—
as one inseparable reality.

Yes, but only in appearance...
We stumble, rise, break, mend.
We love in innocently confused ways.
We pass on that of which we are unaware.

And still, beneath every habit, every wound,
every joy, every woe, there is something untouched.

Something timeless and innocent.
Something that cannot be harmed.
Something that remembers what we seemingly forget.
Inner Peace beyond all mental understanding.

This book is a return to that.

A slow unbinding.
A soft recognition.
A humble bow to the presence
that lives beneath every inherited weight.

It ends with me-ME...
because, it must end in the place where truth begins.

In the quiet center of Mysterious Existence.
Myterious Existence that has
always been...

Always here.

Everpresent.

Waiting to be graciously met.
Invited.
Welcomed.

Lovingly acknowledged.

If you listen gently,
but not with ears...
you may feel it too.

The hush beneath your thoughts.
The spark inside your chest.
The everpresent original YOU
prior to name and form
that has never been broken.

This is the meeting.
The communion.
A benediction of sorts.
A divine marriage, if you will.

Preface

This is the inevitable unraveling unto truth.
This is the apparent remembrance
that what ended with you
is what begins with you too.

Welcome home.

Welcome to true self-discovery!

We are not born lacking.
We are born as presence itself—
as love itself.

Whole.
Open.
Unbroken.

Joyous. Happy. Free.

A child does not need to learn love.
They *are* love—

until the habits, fears,
and wounds of those before them
begin to innocently veil that truth.

What we inherit is not our loving essence.
What we inherit are the shadows:
the resistance,
the avoidance,
the unspoken grief.

The judgments and fears.

And of course,
traits and other concepts
that are fascinatingly beneficial
for a time.

However, mostly...
what we have adopted and assumed
are behaviors and beliefs
passed down as survival,
as self-preservation,
innocently mistaken for love.

And so the child learns not who they are,
but who the parent could not yet be.
They learn to deny experience of
what is happening here-now.

Innocently turning away from
what the body-mind is sensing,
perceiving, feeling, thinking,
saying, and acting.

Creating filters, masks, and stories
about what experience is "supposed to"
or "not supposed" to be.
Effectively falling asleep
to our natural spontaneous
aliveness and wholeness.

Creating illusory distance,
a false sense of separation.
Innocently becoming attached
to patterns that protect,
and defend what one is not.

Habits that mentally and emotionally imprison.

Yet even here—
love that needs no reason is never lost.
It patiently awaits beneath the layers.

Unconditional love is always shining...
in laughter, in trust.
Even amid the pain and hurt...
Even when trusting mistrust—it is here.

Unconditional love shines in the way a child
still already knows—beyond belief and assumptions.
Prior to belief and assumptions.
Prior to untrue self-images and self-concepts.
Beyond mental masks we assume ourselves to be.

Rumi wrote,

"The wound is where the light enters."

This book is not about teaching love.

Not about trying to be something
you were told to be.

It is about Remembrance.

But not remembering with the mind's memory.
Remembering prior to mind and all experience.

Somehow remembering you ARE loving presence.

Unlearnable.
Unshakable.
Timeless.
Eternal.

Before attaching labels, memories,
concepts and stories to who I think I AM.

Introduction

When we lovingly,
and willingly,
and consciously,
acknowledge what apparently
blocks our deepest truths,
true self-awareness exposes
what one really is…

ME as mysterious existence, itSELF.

This book then becomes
a sacred meeting with what we have carried—
the habits, the wounds, the unspoken weight—
the magnificence that we are—
and choosing... this:
not to pass on what only burdens.

Not through perfectionism.
Not through more performance.
Not through self-hate or self-punishment.

But through presence, authenticity,
and our natural sacred inner qualities.

Through humility. Through compassion.
Through truth. Through grace.
Through infinite patience.

And unending gratitude and trust.

To be a conscious and
unconditionally loving parent
is not to mold another life.

It is to walk alongside a living presence
that reflects back the one you have always been.

This is the apparent work.
This is the grace of healing.
This is the invitation:

It can end with "me."

And something freer, quieter,
infinitely whole, primally innocent
can awaken in them.

In YOU.

In ME.

All at once.

As all are one.

1

Inheritance of Wounds

The ache we carry is not always ours.
But it becomes ours
when we choose not to look.

The deepest wounds a child carries
are those of an unhealed parent.

Not necessarily the wounds made by hands,
but by absences, or unconscious speech
or behavior reflecting unattended grief,
fear, and hurt from those who raised us.

By the constrained love that was too
entangled in sorrow or confusion to shine.
By the gaze that looked,
but did not see... itSELF.

A child's mind does not know to call it grief.

And doesn't have too.
But within, an essence senses
that something important
seems to be missing—

So they make themselves smaller.
Quieter. Easier to hold.

Playing the game of trying to appease...
placate... adapt to...
the parent. Everyone. Society.

Hoping that maybe, this time,
they will finally be a "good boy" or "good girl."
Entertaining fantasies of inner torment.

But the parent, too, was once a child.
They, too, built mental walls around
their own heart, innocently so—
trying to fit in—
when loving presence was eclipsed
by unhealed wounds of *their* parents.

Inheritance of Wounds

They grew up thinking survival was love.
That enmeshment was love.
That trying to "fit-in" was love.
That clinging to the mind's endless
rationalizations is the way.

That creating an unworthy self-concept was safe.

That fragmenting our inner reality meant peace.

So what is passed down is not always wisdom.
Sometimes, it is the ache of generations
who didn't know how to speak
and feel what hurt them.

A legacy of unshed tears.
Of avoidance.
Of unfinished healing.

Yet—
what wounds in silence
can also mend in silence.

Remember once more what Rumi said…

"The wound is where the light enters."

What was broken in darkness
can still be mended in light.

The healing light of awareness.

When the grown child pauses, listens,
breathes, and chooses differently—
not to blame,
but to understand—

To look inward with loving
compassion and infinite tenderness
the thought patterns and mental habits begin to wane.

Slowly. Gently.
Like dawn through heavy fog.
Innocent veils lifting.

This is not rebellion.
This is effortless power more freeing
than mentally masking ourselves—

Again and again and again.

This is Grace. A homecoming.

To self. To truth. To love.

Unconditional love always
waiting beneath the mental noise.

Everpresent.

2

Recognition and Reverence

To see the child as they are
is to see beyond names,
into the place where love is everpresent.

Here. Now.
Within and without.

There comes a moment—
rare, but possible—
when a parent sees their child
not as *theirs*, but as *them*.

Not in the mirror of features or gestures.
Not in shared temperaments or tastes.
Not in the lineage of stories or genetic offspring
or the echo of surnames.

But in something deeper.

Wordless. Timeless. Formless.

The still presence beneath all becoming.

They look into the child's eyes
and no longer see a smaller version of themselves,
or someone to mold,
or fix,
or guide.

They see unconditional love
reflecting themself.

Life.

The same breath that moves through them.

And for the first time,
they fall to their knees—
not out of duty or obligation,
but in awe.

Recognition and Reverence

To love a child this way
is to see beyond
the illusion of separation.

To realize:

This one did not come *from* me.
This one came *through* the idea of "me."

And I, too, as a body-mind,
came through something greater.

Am something beyond an
apparent body-mind-complex
mascarading as an identity.

The child or grandchild is not a project.

Not an extension.
Not a second chance.
Not a possession.
Not even a reason to be happy.

They are the mirror of grace itself—
returned in small form
to remind us who we are
beneath our forgetting.

When the parent sees this—
truly sees—becomes aware...
they weep.

Not from sadness,
but from the unbearable tenderness
of recognition.

Infinite reverie...

They touch the child's face
and touch their own soul.

They speak gently,
not because they were taught to,
but because reverence has no other voice.

And in this sacred seeing,
all inheritance dissolves.

What once seemed broken
is no longer passed down.

What was seemingly withheld now flows.

Nothing else needs to be taught.

Only acknowledged. Remembered. Allowed to breathe.

3

The Mirror and the Self

The child does not reflect
who you wish to be.
They reflect what you have
not yet made peace with.

The child does not just reflect light.
They reflect all of you.

The parts you love.
The parts you hid.
The parts you swore you
had buried long ago.

Their rage might feel too familiar.
Their wonder might feel too distant.
Their fear might echo something
unresovled in your own body.

And so the child becomes
not just a mirror—but a teacher.

Not by trying. Just by being.

They pull forth the parent you are,
and the one you once needed.
They summon the unhealed,
the unfinished, the unspoken.

The secrets we are afraid of exposing.

Every reaction becomes a revelation.
Every moment, a choice—
To pass down what was passed to you,
or to pause, and offer something new.

This is not the love of romance.
And not necessarily soft focus
and sweet bedtime light.
It is fierce grace, uncomfortable at times…

Yet real.

The Mirror and the Self

Because when the child
cries in a way that shakes
something old in you—
that is the mirror.

When they challenge what
you believed was true—but isn't,
that is the mirror.

When they love you with wild,
unwounded trust—
that is the mirror, too.

They don't just show you who *they* are.
They show you who *you* still are
beneath the mental armor.
Beneath layers of unnecessary defense.

And if you're willing—
not perfect, just willing—
you begin to meet yourself again,
not as you imagined you'd be,
but as you always were—are.

Not because of them.
But through them.

As them.

4

The Sacred Undoing

What breaks in you when
you truly love—unconditionally—
is not your strength
but your certainty.

*There is a breaking-down as
a breaking-through that comes
with parenthood—not loud, not tragic.*

A quiet unraveling.
Not of life, but of the false
selves you're innocently projecting.
And niavely protecting.

The plans you had.
The image you held.
The tidy beliefs about who you are,
and how love should or should not look.

All of it begins to slip.
You think you are here to shape them.
But they shape you.
Not by force—by presence.

By needing you in ways you didn't expect.
By *not* matching the story
you wrote before they arrived.

And so begins the sacred undoing.
The ego—the false self—once certain,
sharp-edged, unconsciously purposeful—
softens, dissolves, begins to trust.

It learns to sit in not-knowing.
To hold space instead of answers.
To abide in love as awareness.

To question in wonderment:

What is the heart asking, now?

Instead of clinging to the mind's favorite questions:

What do I want? What's in it for me?

To compassionately, yet courageously
and patiently ask:

Who am I, really?

Instead of:

*How do I extract my happiness and
worthiness from my child or grandchild.*

This is not weakness.
This is grace.
The kind that comes only when love for *your*
inner well-being matters more than control.

Than anything.

You stop performing the
role of "parent" and start
simply showing up—as human,
as heart, as friends,
what you really are,
as presence.

Infinitely tender and loving presence.

And in this sacred allowing, you realize:

Your strength was never in
your rules of self-oppression.
It was in your willingness to listen.
To bend.
To effortlessly sway like a tree in the wind.
To remain open even when it hurts.

Especially when it hurts.

This is not the parent you imagined.
Or could ever imagine.
This is the parent or grandparent you become
when you let go of trying to become anything.

When you see the innocent futility
of trying to be the perfect parent.
And set aside the illusory fear
of being a bad parent.

No gold stars here.
No blueprint needed.
No perfect end because
all of this is already perfect.

All that remains is this:

Life's infinite innocence.

This moment.

Love big enough to unmake you—

Infinite enough to break the ideas
of who or what you *think* and *believe* you are—

And still be home.

5

The Healing Spiral

Some things are passed down.
Others are set down—laid to rest.
And that is where it begins to change.

Wounds do not begin with you.
They arrive quietly,
wrapped in innocent ignorance,
carried not by choice but by habit—
unspoken fears, old blame, half-lived love.

They move from parent to
child not through malice,
but through forgetting.

Forgetting who we are beneath the noise.
Forgetting that love is not
something we must create—
but something we seemingly return to.

Seemingly because the love we seek,
the love we are—

Is everpresent.

And then—a child is born.
An empty canvas of unconditional love.
Not waiting to be painted.
Not needing to be told what it is.

But whole.
Radiant.
Unprogrammed.

As they always have been…

Everpresent unconditional loving joyous presence.

They do not need to be taught love.

They *are* love.

Joy that doesn't need to be named—misinterpreted.

Freedom that hasn't yet been tamed—
or doesn't need to be.

They smile, and something timeless in you stirs.

Not because they are learning from you,
but because they are *reminding* you.

OF YOU.

You see what you once were—yet still are.

Seemingly hiding under the conditioning,
Under the judgments,
under the voices in your mind.
Untrue voices telling you
who you have to be.

And in that seeing,
you are given a divine chance:
Not to teach love,
but to unlearn everything that masks it.

To set down what was
unconsciously handed to you,
and refuse to carry it forward.

Not out of hate or resentment or blame.

But as primal innocence seeing itself.

This is the spiral both downward and upward.
A gentle return to the center you never left—
again and again—
each time with more clarity,
more softness, more truth.

You may believe you must be perfect.

But presence doesn't require perfection.
Only willingness.
Only remembering.

And as you move differently,
speak differently,
hold differently—
something shifts, quietly but forever.

One day, without trying,
your child may turn to you,
not to say "you taught me love,"
but simply to shine with the love they never had to hide.

And you'll know:
not that you gave them something,
but that you can't protect love…

Because THEY are love.

Because YOU are love.

Because...

Love is the only thing that needs no protection.

6

Love as Presence

There is no fixing here.
Only abiding.
Only remaining as you are.
Only love, without instruction—no rules.

In the end,
there is nothing to teach.
Nothing to mold.
Nothing to become.

Only this:
To be as you already are.
To be.

To sit on the floor with your child,
not to instruct them with
egoic motives—to find
your happiness in them.

And not to improve them
so you feel better about yourself,
but to join them—
As equals.

To hold their sadness without solving it.
To embrace their confusion without judging it.
To witness their joy without needing to name it.
To walk beside them without rushing ahead.
To love them without confining them to...
unhelpful labels and categories.

Because love is not a strategy.
It is not a performance.
It is not earned, built, or perfected.

In fact, true unconditional love is effortless.
Already and always perfect.
Love is what remains when
you stop trying to be something you are not.

When you stop efforting to
be the programming you were taught.

Love as Presence

And presence—
true presence—
is how love speaks without words.

A soft eye. Kind eyes.
A still hand. Kind hands.
A breath that only speaks in silence.

You are not here to be the hero or martyr.
Or the victim or rescuer or persecutor.
Not to be saved or
be the savior of your "child."

You are not here to write their story.
Or your own—
through them—
as your human clown.

You are here to keep the lamp lit
as YOU find YOUR own way home.

To the home YOU never left—within.

The child is not waiting for anything.
They are simply here to be.

And this beingness happens
not through doing—

but through allowing, surrendering—letting go.

Being here.
Being now.
Being real.

Not always perfectly calm.
Not always wise.
But deeply honest.

By openly admitting you're confused.
That you don't know.
That you actually don't know much at all.

Yet remaining open.
Available.
Alive.

Because in the quiet presence of love,
there is no fear.
There is no lack.
There is no hidden or personal agenda.

There is only this moment—
holy in its ordinariness.
Enough in its simplicity.

Humorous in its innocent absurdity.

Freeing in our capacity to laugh at ourselves...

Alive with grace.

And that...
is everything.

The nothingness that is everything.
The everything that is nothingness.

As the divine cosmic godly
comedic play of existence unfolds.

7

The Guest We Cannot Keep

You are not love because of them.
You are love with them.
As them.
And before them.
And after.

Love is all there is.

Yet there appears a guest in the house of the heart.
They arrive with small feet, bright eyes, wings not yet
formed, and a laughter that feels like salvation.
Or, redemption.

You let them in—of course you do.
You build your world around them.
You rearrange your days, your priorities,
even the way the breath moves
through your body.

You say it's love.
And it *is*.
A type of limited love, however,
when you forget that you
are them and they are you.

So… quietly, something else begins to happen.

The guest becomes the reason you smile.
The reason you feel worthy.
The reason you forgive yourself.
The reason you believe you are lovable.
The reason you are here.

Without meaning to,
you hand them the keys
to your joy and self-worth.
And meaning and purpose.

And without realizing it,
you begin to enmesh, innocently calling it love.
They become your mirror—

but not the kind that shows truth.
The kind that shows who
you wish you were.
Who you hope to be.

You say,

My child is my everything.

But what if they *aren't* meant to be…
Your everything?

What if YOU already were everything
before they ever arrived?

What if YOU already *are*
the everything YOU are seeking?

The child is *not* here to
fill the place in you
that *your* parents never reached.

They are *not* here to
complete the story
you didn't get to live.

They are *not* here to fill the
void of your unhealed wounds.

For a third time, Rumi spoke,

"The wound is where the light enters."

So don't use your child
as your band-aid.
As your emotional outlet.

They are not here to
be your wholeness.
They are a guest.

A sacred one.

But still—a guest.
As is the apparent you,
you believe yourself to be.

And one day, they will leave.

Not in absence,
but in becoming.

They will grow, pull back,
step into their own center.

And fly...

With or without you.

The Guest We Cannot Keep

And if you have made them your
center, your everythng,
you will collapse when
their physical presence departs.

But if you remember—
that the love they
seemed to give you
was only ever a reflection
of the love already within you—
then their departure will
not dishearten you.

It will free you. It will be a joyful celebration!

Because you are not love *because* of them.

You are love *with* them.
And before them.
And after.

Let the guest be held,
but not mistaken
for the truth everpresent within.

Let the child be loved,
but not turned into
the reason you are enough.

You were enough before
you opened the door.

You will still be,
when it closes.

As are they—
Infinitely enough,
whole, complete, worthy, already.

Yes...
yes...
and yes...
so are you...

Already lacking nothing—ever.

Before the experience
of "my child" arose,
and during—and after.

All experience is fleeting, impermanent.
Like waves in an
ocean of love that rush
from your fingertips,
when grasped or clung too.

Know that nothing stays the same.
Not even for an instant.
That is your freedom.

The freedom to give yourself permission to relax.

The freedom to allow your experience to be as it is.

The freedom not to take life so seriously.

That is your freedom.

Their freedom.

Freedom itself.

Freedom to be free or free to be bound.

8

Like the Sun Loves the Flower

The sun does not cling to the bloom.
It gives light, and never holds on.

The tree does not ask
the sapling to grow in its image.
It gives shade, shelter, and space—
then lets the young branches
stretch however they will.

The river does not direct the path of the stream.
It simply flows, offering movement, not instruction.

Simple grace of being.

And the sun—
the sun loves the flower
with a kind of generosity
that never asks the
petals to open faster,
or in a different color.

It warms.
It waits.
It trusts.

This is the kind of love nature knows.

Effortless.
Unattached.
Whole.

A giving that needs nothing in return.

Let us remember—we ARE nature.

And too, let us remember this:
Unconditional love is NOT a transaction.
Is not a give and take relationship.

Unconditional love is always one way.
Like the sun—always shining
without concern upon whom it shines.

Like the Sun Loves the Flower

What if parenthood was like this?
What if human life *is* like this?
Not forced intstruction pressed onto the child,
but a field they are free to run through.

Not a sculptor chiseling away,
but soft rain soaking into the soil
so something alive can grow,
blossom and mature.

To love like the sun is to
stop gripping, clinging, craving.

To love like the river is to
release control.
Rather, the illusion of control.

To love like the tree is to
know they may never grow
the way you imagined—
and that is not a failure.

That is the miracle.

Because they are not here
to fulfill your hopes, dreams, expectations.

BUT TO DESTROY THEM.

They are here to become
who they already are.

And your role?
Not to unconsciously,
reactively mold,
but to consciously nourish.

Not to forcefully direct,
but to delight—
in the mystery, paradox, and awe.

To be the ever-loving presence
that gives freely,
and then steps back—
not out of indifference,
but out of...

Grace.

Out of compassionate understanding
that life is sacred.

All life.

Not to be pushed, controlled, manipulated.

Love like that doesn't bind.

It blesses without even knowing it.

And leaves the gate wide open as it always is.

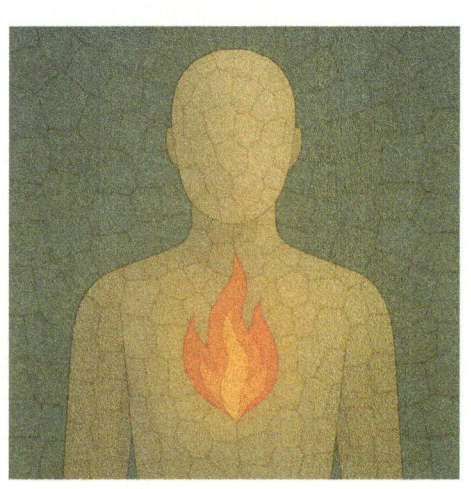

9

The Flame Inside the Form

The child is not here to become divine.
They are here to remind you you already are.

*Before the child speaks, they **know**.*
*Before they are taught, they **are**.*

Already whole. Worthy.
Already complete. Enough.

Silent with the kind of
joyous wisdom that cannot
be written down.

Or given.

This joyous grace shows
in the way they look at clouds.
In the way they ask a
question without needing an answer.

In the way they forgive,
instantly, fully,
as if nothing ever happened—
because in truth, it didn't.

Not in the place they live from—
here-now.
This is not innocence in the
way we use the word—
it is presence.

Everpresent Loving Awareness.
Infinite Tenderness.

Unfiltered.
Unbroken.
Unforgotten.

We attempt to protect the child from harm.
We attempt to guide them through the world.
But underneath all that doing,
there is something we must remember:

The Flame Inside the Form

Love needs no protection or defense.

True love is unwoundable—
incapable of condition.

Which reminds us…

They are not here to be *made* whole and worthy.
They are here to *remind us* that we already are.

The child is not the beginning of a life.
They are the continuation of the timeless—
a flame moving through form,
carrying the same light that lives in us
beneath the layers of unnecessary identity.

Beneath the unattended shame and guilt.

To see the child truly
is not to measure their gifts,
or merly marvel at their potential,
or praise their beauty.

It is to bow.

Not in front of them,
but within yourself.
To the presence that looks
back through their eyes—

presence that has no name,
no age, no beginning.
And no end.

This is not metaphor or myth.
This is not another story or narrative.
This is what you sense deep within.

And their overwhelming expressive joy?
And their spontaneous aliveness?
And their innocent honesty
before we mask it with our own judgments?

It is what stops you mid-sentence
when they say something
too true for their age.
It is not that it is too true.

It is just *true*.

And in that moment, you remember:
They are not becoming divine.
They are divine, as are you.
Arising from the only divinity there *is*.

The infinite cosmic reality underneath it all.
The only difference is they
have not yet learned to forget.

Like what happened to you.

So don't help them forget.

Or remember...
because they already are.

Hold them gently. Tenderly.
Speak to them honestly, kindly, lovingly.
Honestly let them continue
their freedom in these words…

I don't know honey except that we are here.

And let their being bring you
back to your inner grace.
Unconditional acceptance.
Unconditional gratitude.
Unconditional joyous appreciation
for the life that you are—for all that is.

The flame of life everpresent does not need to be lit.

Only *not* mentally veiled by our innocent ignorance.
The innocent ignoring of what is asking for tender and gracious feeling, healing, awakening.

Within.

10

The Door Is Still Open

Even if you believe you
have tried too hard.
Even if you believe you
have disappeared.

Even if you believe you didn't know how—
you can still lovingly direct your attention back to
the loving presence that...
you already are.

Your everpresent loving awareness—
the Real You.

It Ends With Me

There is more than one kind of absence.
Some parents leave.
Others stay—
but never truly arrive.

They do everything…
seemingly.
Say the right things…
apparently.
Plan the perfect birthdays…
so they feel good about themselves.

Show up to every event,
camera in hand, smile rehearsed.
They feel as if they give all of themselves—

And if that is so…

That means they even give
the parts still hurting,
wounded, unconscious.

The parts they've never faced.
The sorrow they packed
away in some deep, silent corner,
hoping love for their child
would be enough to keep it hidden.

But wounds do not disappear
just because we try harder.
They find other ways to surface.

In the pressure to be a "better parent."
In the fear of failure.
In the overprotectiveness.
In the smothering.
In the overbearing.

Even when we rationalize NOT
attending to their apparent needs.

Yet, often, unknowingly,
we transfer energies to them…

Anxiety. Shame. Guilt. And so on.

In our worry that we innocently
misinterpret as love.
In the unnecessary and unhelpful
worry that only drives them away.

Worry that masks our inner beauty and graceful calm.
Worry that seems to drive our inner peace and
inseparable connection to the divine away.

And the child feels it.

Not always in words—
but in the subtle tension, arising
from the seeming unreachable places
within ourselves.

In the sense that something
untrue is being asked of them
without ever being said.

So confusion persists, in both of you.
Because when a parent hasn't
tended to their own pain,
they can mistake the child as the cure.

More innocent confusion ensues.

Often as parents we try to *earn*
worthiness through parenting.
To fix our past by attempting to
perfect the present.

To be everything we didn't receive—
without realizing we are still
bleeding beneath the effort.

But no amount of doing can
heal what hasn't been faced,
lovingly acknowledged.

The Door Is Still Open

No performance of love can
replace the effortless,
needless presence of uncondtional love,
already here...
Everpresent.

And still—
it is not too late.
Whether you left or stayed,
hidden behind a mask,
whether you clung too tightly
or kept your distance—

There is always a moment to stop.

To return.
To meet the child as they are now.
To meet yourself as you are now.

To say:

I was trying so hard, I forgot to feel.
I gave everything but my authenticity.

OR

I felt too ashamed to share
what I knew in my heart was available.

And I lovingly choose differently now.

You cannot go back in time.
But you can go deeper.

Into honesty.
Into loving presence.
Into compassionate understanding
that doesn't posture or perform or react,
but simply *is*.

They may not meet you **here** right away.
They may not know how.
That's okay.

Because healing is not something you demand.

And the truth is this:

Your healing is yours and yours alone,
with or without them.

A "Healing Presence" is something
you become the moment you stop
hiding from your own sorrow.

When "you" stop avoiding, deflecting,
judging, running away...

The Door Is Still Open

You become safe to love again.

And be loved, without limits, without condition.

No longer through fear.

Or need.
Or guilt.

But through grace.

And the door—
the one you thought
had closed long ago—
is still open.

It always was.

It only took loving awareness.
Kind awareness.
Tender awareness.

Awareness. Awareness. Awareness.

11

What If I Don't Know?

The moment you stop
pretending to know
is the moment you become
safe enough to love and be loved.

There is a quiet truth many
parents carry but are too afraid to say:

I don't know what I'm doing.
I don't know what's right.
I don't know who I am.
And... that's okay.

The world told us we had to know.
That love meant certainty.
That leadership meant answers.
That to guide a child,
we had to know everything.

So we pretended.
Creating more false identities.

We filled the silence with
advice and false beliefs.
We clung to rules that oppress.
We performed the unconscious
ritual instead of being effortlessly authentic—
perfectly natural.

But eventually—
something gives way.
Hurts so much we
can no longer hide.

The mental armor and emotional cocoon
we have built around the heart
feels too constrictive.

Finally, we hear...
Something screaming or
delicately asking for loving attention.

Not in failure, but in mercy.

You sit across from your child and realize:

They are not asking for perfection.
They are asking for presence...
Loving Presence.

They don't need a hero.

They only need unconditional love—
loving freedom.

And in that moment,
the most honest love
may sound like this:

I don't know who I am yet.
I thought I had to teach
you everything, but
maybe we're here to learn together.

I thought I was supposed
to shape you, but maybe
you're here to help me
remember what's real.

This possibility is not a collapse
of reality but of falsehood.

It's not surrendering authority
but of that no longer serving.
It's surrendering ego—
personal identity—
the false psychological selves
vying for dominion.

It's the sacred humility
of stepping off the pedestal
and sitting beside your child
with both feet on the ground.

Not above. Not ahead. With.

A giveless and takeless love.

From this place, love is no longer separation.
It is inseparable presence.

An unsolvable mystery you *are*... together.

And strangely—
miraculously—
miraculous as everything already is...
when you admit you don't know,
the space within you,
and between you and the
apparent other, your child, opens.

What If I Don't Know?

Now there is spaciousness to listen.
A mysterious inseparable space for truth.
Space for the child to be who they are—
not who you imagined.

And for you to become
someone new,
again and again.

Moment by moment by moment by moment.

Situation unknown.

And that's okay.

To be as you already are.

Not by knowing more.

But in the graceful release of *not knowing*.

Just this moment.
Just this breath.
Just being here together, as one…
without answers—
but with everything that matters.

As Timeless Loving Presence.

Everpresent Loving Awareness.

The source of all existence.

The real YOU.

12

It Ends With Me

I no longer choose to carry
what was handed to me.

*I lovingly acknowledge it.
I bless it. Befriend it…
And effortlessly lay it down,
with kindhearted understanding.*

I was born into stories I didn't choose.
Innocent wounds I didn't see.
Patterns so old they naively
claimed to be the voice of truth.
But not true at all.

So I carried them.
Not because I wanted to—
but because no one had shown me how to let go.

Until now.

Not perfectly.
Not all at once.

But with awareness.
With breath.
With love.

By lovingly acknowledging
my primal innocence.

I looked at what I didn't want to see.

And it's okay.

I felt what had been passed over for years.

And it's okay.

I stopped running.
I stopped blaming.

And stayed.

It Ends With Me

Calmly remained with my inner situation.
Feelings, sensations, behaviors,
thoughts, ideas, judgments,
loves, hates, all of it.

I abided within when it got uncomfortable.
I remained with experience
when I didn't have answers.
When prayers, hopes, rationalizations,
and wishful thinking stopped working.

I stopped believing thoughts were absolutely true.

I stayed when the "pain" asked for
more than what the mind thought it could bear.

And in abiding attention within,
I remembered—what love really is.

For the last time, Rumi illuminated,

"The wound is where the light enters."

And so I graciously placed all of the light
of kind and gentle and loving attention
on the seeming wounds—
on the apparent resistance
to prove what Rumi spoke.

Not to control.
Not to sacrifice.
Not to perfect or change
or modify or mask
or manipulate experience.

But to become aware of
what lies beneath all that
I have been avoiding.

Presence.
Stillness.
Infinite unconditional love.

Timeless love so vast and unending
it allows for every possibility.

A love willing to see—everything.
To feel everything.
To allow everything.

So, I see now...

Not with the eyes, but through them.

I am aware...

The child was never the one to fix.

They were the one who reminded me
of what I had seemingly forgotten.

That I am whole.

Always was... is.

That I am not the past.

Never was... not even for a moment.

That I am not the voice
in the mind that says, *not enough*.

That I don't need to pass on
what has outlived its temporary usefulness.

That I can stop.
Consciously choose to stop.

Here. Now.

With this breath.
With this choice.

The wound continues only if I carry it.

That is clear.

And I won't.

I choose to effortlessly
let all that no longer serves…
innocently move along.

Not because I hate where I came from,
Or hate what the body-mind is saying,
doing or feeling…

But because I finally understand. Am aware.

And the infinite tenderness of
love is enough to let it rest.

So when my child looks into my eyes,
they will not see the echo of my pain.
They will see the loving presence that held it all—

That is choosing something new.
This is the inheritance I leave.

Not legacy.
Not the harsh judgment of perfectionism.
But a tender-hearted path that does not repeat.

Patterns of consciousness laid to
rest in the unending lap of love.

It ends with me.

And something else—
something freer, fuller, quieter—
begins with them.

And in this ending—
this simultaneous beginning...
I see what was true all along:
neither of us were ever broken.

Only seemingly covered by innocent misperceptions.

Those mental veils and stories
of mind—believed in—
that were not true…

Not true, absolutely.

Neither I nor my child need
to be fixed because, yes, "no one was ever broken."

This inner freedom only took
acknowledgement of my primal innocence,
unattended sorrow, and my unforgotten
gifts and sacred qualities holding steady in my heart.

In this seeing... truth prevails.

Not my stories of truth,
nor expectations,
or any ideas of the like…

But timeless unconditional non mental truth…

That we are already whole, infinitely innocent.

Unshakably Complete.

Inseparably Enough.

Lacking nothing.

That **I AM** That.

As are ALL children—
ALL parents—all of us.

All life—EVERYTHING!

Unconditional loving presence itself.

Always were. Always was. Always are.

Here.

Now.

As the Universe Expressing itself to itself for itself...

As itSELF...

In this great mystery...

Playing the divine master game of life...

Over and over and over and over and over and over...

About the Author

A Symbol of Loving Awareness

The name on the cover—Peace President—does not refer to a single person, but to a presence within all of us.

It is symbolic of our innermost sacred nature: the Infinite Compassion, Infinite Welcoming, Infinite Patience, and Infinite Humility that live quietly at the core of every human being—Loving Awareness.

In this sense, this book is written by you—all of us—as a loving reflection of the Infinite YOU.

Peace President is an archetype emerging in human consciousness to assist in the great shift now unfolding within us all: from self-preservation to shared purpose, from fear and division to the higher possibility of being consciously human and unconditionally loving.

It points toward an undivided sense of self that knows no separation, no division, no blame, no hatred, and no aggression—only Infinite Love, unconditionally and infinitely expressed.

Grace that knows no bounds—only truth beyond belief.

About the Author

A Symbol of Loving Awareness

The name on the cover—Peace President—does not refer to a single person, but to a presence within all of us.

It is symbolic of our innermost sacred nature: the Infinite Compassion, Infinite Welcoming, Infinite Patience, and Infinite Humility that live quietly at the core of every human being—Loving Awareness.

In this sense, this book is written by you—all of us—as a loving reflection of the Infinite YOU.

Peace President is an archetype emerging in human consciousness to assist in the great shift now unfolding within us all: from self-preservation to shared purpose, from fear and division to the higher possibility of being consciously human and unconditionally loving.

It points toward an undivided sense of self that knows no separation, no blame, no hatred, and no aggression—only Infinite Love, unconditionally and infinitely expressed.

Grace that knows no bounds—only truth beyond belief.

Coming Next from the Peace President Collection

Peace President and the New Earth Dream Team
What Conscious and Loving Government Looks Like

A visionary call to awaken conscious leadership and sacred citizenship.

This powerful guide invites readers to reclaim their inner voice and sacred authority, embody the unifying inner qualities that transcend division, and discover what truly works—and what doesn't—for building a life of shared prosperity, conscious leadership, and collective thriving as one undivided humanity.

Coming January 2026

PeacePresidentUnited.org

Acknowledgments

Let us begin by acknowledging
the Great Mystery—
this wildly beautiful and bewildering
dream called life in which we find
ourselves. The unseen Source of all
creation, from which every thought,
form, and experience arises.

Let us acknowledge the essence of our
innermost being—
what we call human consciousness—
and its infinite capacity for undivided
loving care, generosity, and compassion
toward one another.

It is through this consciousness that life
becomes aware of itself—and through love,
that awareness finds its highest expression.

Let us acknowledge, with tenderness and
humility, our bodies—these extraordinary
vessels through which the miracle of
experience unfolds. Through the senses we
touch, see, feel, and remember.

Through the felt sense of experience that we call the body, we learn what it means to be human, and through its resilient fragility, we are reminded of what it means to be alive.

Let us honor what appears as the other—
the illusion of separation we have so often mistaken for truth. May we recognize that every encounter, every seeming division, is an invitation to remember our shared origin—to see ourselves, again and again, in one another.

And ultimately, let us acknowledge that it is perfectly all right not to know.
To live with the simple, freeing honesty of "I don't know."

From this humility, true wisdom begins.
From this stillness, understanding awakens.
From this surrender, peace takes form.

May these acknowledgments serve as both offering and remembrance:
that the journey of awakening belongs to no one and to all—and that...

Even in our unknowing—we are already home.

www.ingramcontent.com/pod-product-compliance
Lightning Source LLC
Chambersburg PA
CBHW040555010526
44110CB00055B/2784